Inequality Unlimited

Two essays and an interview for economic justice and accountability

by

Glenn Brigaldino

© 2013

Introduction

It is hardly news anymore, if it ever was, that a tiny minority of people control an enormously disproportionate share of society's wealth. The 'rest of us' those people one could classify as "the 99%", find it harder and harder to make ends meet. Money is power one knows, but while in the past it might have been possible for average wage earners and their families to climb up the social ladder, nowadays many people are barely holding on, constantly fearing to completely fall off the ladder. In many places, there is simply no ladder.

What causes society to become more and more unjust, in a seemingly irreversible manner? To start with, there are deep democratic deficits, weak accountability structures and unrepresentative political systems that often constrain or even prevent citizen participation in the public sphere. Where citizens have no voice, the political system is operated and manipulated by governments and regimes (and of course the individuals who control the institutions and the corporations) injustice rules, whether openly or covert, or in both forms (just think of the NSS and what it may or may not have done with all the illegally obtained personal information it has gathered from people near and far, friends and foes alike).

In many countries which were once categorized as 'advanced' or developed', the political system works in favour of the rich. How many of these individuals got rich to start with, is seldom asked, but it is safe to assume that few gained their wealth and fortunes through honest work. The fact remains, where wealth is gained by unfair means and on the backs of the poor, social divisions become entrenched, societies become polarized.

This publication consists of two essays on social inequality and an interview conducted with non-conformist professor of economics. All three contributions were published in 2013 with "Newtopiamagazine" (and can be viewed there in the archives section), an online venture that functions as a place where a versatile group of individuals express their views and experiences within a structure of respected peers. These three articles are brought together here in a format that allows the reader to access them as a unit. As a bonus of sorts for accessing this material this way, two unpublished short letters to the editors of Harper's magazine (one addressing an economic and the other, a civil rights matter) are added at the end.

The first two essays deal with today's manifestations of inequality. They are presented here in reverse order of publication, as "Far from Fed" is an extension of the research and argument made in "Crumbs of capitalism for you and me". The interview with John Weeks (technically an exchange of online communications and various draft responses that were mutually edited and agreed upon), seeks to recapture economic argument for progressive thought.

Conservative commentators and mainstream economists tend to dispute that the capitalist system is the root causes for growing income disparities on a global scale. Often they go to great lengths to make the case for the legitimacy of a globalised economic order that produces enormous wealth for the few, while hundreds of millions in all countries of the world struggle to secure a nutritious daily meal for themselves and their children.

It is a dishonest and disrespectful case, one that chooses to ignore, least of all attempt to explain how "The world's 1,226 billionaires have more combined wealth than 3.5 billion people – half the entire planet's population. The richest 10 percent of the world's population takes 90 percent of the world's income (http://www.fpif.org/articles/changing_the_rules).

In a 2012 article on trends in global food security following the 2008 economic crises I observed that "global food security must be seen as a core element of an overall global social crises resulting from a continued laissez faire approach to socio-economic development, alongside eroded democratic institutions and representation mechanisms, notably in the core capitalist countries." (a)

Many of the sources and arguments captured and made in that article are closely linked to how inequality manifests itself throughout the world. Together with the essays presented here, while they do stand on their own, this material becomes much more powerful as a source of knowledge and insight when the many quoted resources are consulted as well.

I hope by having condensed this important material and by trying to put it in a practical context, the reader will feel more informed, maybe even empowered to challenge many of the so-called 'official wisdoms' or what passes as 'common sense' in political, social, environmental and economic debate.

Ottawa, October 2013

a)   'Between Gourmet Dinners and Ration Cards' Cards, is available as a Kindle e-book, but can also be downloaded for free at: http://papers.ssrn.com/sol3/papers.cfm?abstract_id=2250849

Far from Fed-up?

© 2013, Glenn Brigaldino

Newtopia-Link: http://newtopiamagazine.wordpress.com/2013/06/15/far-from-fed-recent-trends-in-inequality

© 2013, Glenn Brigaldino

On a late May morning on my way to work, I noticed this huge armoured truck through the bus window. It was one of those grey, heavy-duty vehicles that you sometimes spot in front of super-markets, collecting the daily cash. This truck however, was about five feet longer than the normal ones as it had double read axles. Easily, a truck like that can carry away twenty tons of your money, I thought. Of course, I have never had any amount worth weighing so it made me wonder whose bags of money were being trucked away in grey anonymity. Regarding the truck itself, specialty customizer companies sell a variety of makes and models of such vehicles. One firm I randomly came across, 'The Armored Group' (http://www.armored-trucks.com) provides 'armored trucks, bulletproof trucks, armored security vehicles, inter-bank vehicles and mobile banking vehicles that meet or exceed the Federal Motor Vehicles Safety Standards (FMVSS).'

It is certainly comforting to know for those whom it may concern, that the vehicles meet safety standards. Perhaps interesting for the light-walleted as well to note that 'Armoured Group' sales offices exist even in places not commonly known as havens of wealth, such as Kenya, Ethiopia and Nigeria. Which leads me to this update to my January article in Newtopia on social inequality (see Newtopia archives: Crumbs of Capitalism). Summer is in sight yes, but economic inequality is not posed to take a summer break. More and more reports have now been published that provide irritable evidence as to the income disparities that are eroding livelihoods and economic opportunities from Detroit to Dhaka.

Norwegian People's Aid, a labour movement humanitarian organisation published an 'Inequality Watch report in September 2012.[i] The report offers useful reading to help comprehend trends and conceptual underpinnings of globalised inequality. Two statements to share here:

- Unequal distribution of power and resources undermine the fundamental values of people's equal rights. It leads to structural oppression of large population groups. It also makes it much harder for poor and marginalized groups to gain political influence. Even if equal rights to vote and participate are formally granted in a highly unequal society, people's real possibilities of political influence will remain limited.

- Resources are available, but extremely unequally distributed. We have also seen that social movements around the world have addressed the issue of inequality and demanded political action for a more just distribution of power, wealth, income, land and access to social services. For years it has been almost impossible to get dominant politicians and development institutions to discuss reduction of inequality or redistribution of resources. Today, we see a slow change, but not yet reflected in consistent new policies.

It is an open secret also the Paris-based Organization for Economic Cooperation and Development (OECD) readily acknowledges: 'wage gaps widened and household income inequality increased in a large majority of OECD countries. This occurred even when countries were going through a period of sustained economic and employment growth."[ii] The OECD goes on to note:

"In OECD countries today, the average income of the richest 10% of the population is about nine times that of the poorest 10% – a ratio of 9 to 1. However, the ratio varies widely from one country to another. It is much lower than the OECD average in the Nordic and many continental European countries, but reaches 10 to 1 in Italy, Japan, Korea, and the United Kingdom; around 14 to 1 in Israel, Turkey, and the United States; and 27 to 1 in Mexico and Chile."

In the "Global Wage Report 2012/13: Wages and Equitable Growth" released by the International Labor Organization in Geneva, differences in wages around the globe are captured and analyzed.[iii] Again unsurprising to the growing number of informed anti-capitalist activists and occupiers, 'real average wage growth has remained far below pre-crisis (2008) levels globally, going into the red in developed economies'. However more telling than wage growth rates and percentages, are the reports' illustrations which reveal just how large the gap now is between labour productivity and wages.

Without a doubt, such gaps are significant and at the individual household and worker level, they are painful to acknowledge and try to come to terms with:

'Between 1999 and 2011 average labour productivity in developed economies increased more than twice as much as average wages. In the United States, real hourly labour productivity in the non-farm business sector increased by about 85 per cent since 1980, while real hourly compensation increased by only around 35 per cent.'

In other, plain words: while the value of what an average worker produced per hour has nearly doubled in just over a decade, only a third of that increase was shared with the worker: capitalists pocketed two thirds. Add to this that workers bear a growing burden of the general tax burden and that businesses, notably large corporations, (presuming they don't succeed to totally circumvent taxes by escaping to tax havens), pay a relatively shrinking share, then the drivers behind the dismal state of economic equality around the world today, become easier to understand.

As a result of a prolonged erosion of wage incomes compared to capital gains and speculation income, maintaining living standards has fallen out of reach for many who used to consider themselves 'middle class'. Few people would readily like to admit this and may rather refuse to identify themselves as new members of the 'lower class' in the capitalist economy. However social circumstances and economic prospects for many who were once considered to be 'white collar' workers, correspond with what used to be the ideal of 'upward mobility. We all know how entire generations of youth in countries such as Spain and Greece, but also in Italy, Portugal and in other countries throughout the European Union, find themselves unemployed for extended periods.

Many have even never been in the workforce at all after high-school, college and university (youth unemployment rates in the 18 of the 27 EU countries hovers above 20%)[iv].

Again, more and more studies are released, including in 2013 'Squeezed: Life in a Time of Food Price Volatility', by the UK-based Institute of Development Studies and Oxfam.[v] The focus here is to demonstrate the failure of wages to keep pace with food price rises and how this is putting a strain on families and communities.

YouTube clip of 'Squeezed' report
https://www.youtube.com/watch?feature=player_embedded&v=HAE-w0W2ikw

Among the key observations from the report, perhaps most discerning are that

- the poorest are eating too little and missing vital nutrients, and
- the urgent need for cash is taking priority over collective social life and values; the high price of essentials is contributing to growing individualism and family nucleation.

These issues are obviously global ones. They may not be openly manifest in wealthier economies, but what inequality and poverty mean when it comes down to chances to lead healthy lives, free from hunger and food insecurity, the parallels between poverty in Alabama, Guatemala or Angola may not be fundamentally different at all. Downward globalization has many dimensions, none pleasant:

"Food safety is a growing concern as families are forced to turn to cheaper, poor quality and sometimes contaminated food to stretch the budget. Increased migration is occurring as people leave rural homes for the city or other countries for more economic opportunities. In Ethiopia, food prices were blamed for people moving to the Middle East.

Heightened family tensions are revealed in increased incidences of domestic violence, alcohol and drug abuse as many men struggle to fulfill their traditional role as the 'breadwinner'. Unpredictable profits and higher costs mean a new generation of farmers is turning to riskier occupations, including gold mining in Burkina Faso and jungle fishing in Bangladesh.

Community life is breaking down as families cut back on important community events such as weddings and funerals in an effort to save money. The squeeze on family budgets is causing women to enter the workforce in ever greater numbers, and grandparents and older daughters are being forced to step in to help with childcare. Families also report skipping meals, foraging or growing their own food. In Bangladesh people are turning to hunger recipes such as 'pantabhat', a watery fermented rice dish."[1]

The myth of social mobility is quickly being replaced by rapidly spreading fear of losing one's' current socio-economic status and resulting limitations in partaking in social and cultural activities. It is now almost an unreal, distant memory that our parents and their parents, embraced the notion that better education directly translates into better jobs, more income, and upward mobility. While there is still some truth in the notion that 'better education pays', it seems to be paying less and less: it is not uncommon today that college and university graduates work in fields which not too long ago only required a solid high school graduation degree.

This point has been well argued in a recent editorial by Jeff Madrick in Harpers' Magazine (http://harpers.org/archive/2013/06/education-is-not-the-answer).
The link made to the world of the capitalist oligarchy is not unsurprising:

"As for the continued success of the One Percent, much of their ongoing gain can be attributed to financialization, as speculation and market-making have surpassed manufacturing as the engine of the American economy. Investment bankers continue to rake in huge bonuses, and CEOs are still plied with stock options, which have soared in value along with the stock market."

To complement the astronomical gains reaped by the few, this current-day 'landed class' is closely linked and interwoven with the realm of politics, where corruption has reached new, unsung heights. Our political institutions have long ceased to genuinely be 'ours': after all, that money rules has been a popular perception long before free-market economies have metamorphosed into a 'free-for-the-rich' system of politically sanctioned corporate immunity.

Under such 'market economy' conditions it is hardly far-fetched to speak of the 'tyranny of the one per cent' as Serge Halimi does in the May 2013 issue of LeMonde diplomatique (http://mondediplo.com/2013/05/01tyranny).[2]

---

[1] See IDS publications at: http://www.ids.ac.uk/idsresearch/food-security

[2] John Holloway's Crack Capitalism (2010) has argued for fostering alternatives by developing autonomous social spaces, within and outside of capitalism. Reviewed at;
http://www.socialistreview.org.uk/article.php?articlenumber=11339

Halimi of course also has numbers to underpin his position, for example that

> "The minimum wage has lost 30% of its value since 1968; there has been no law to facilitate setting up a union in a workplace, despite Obama's campaign promise; work is still taxed twice as heavily as wealth, 39.6% versus 20%".

Yet more importantly, Halimi provides reassurance to inequality opponents and critiques when he sees emancipatory potentials and avenues for constructive dissent and change.

> "Illuminating the real workings of what happens, the mechanisms through which wealth and power have been captured by a minority who control both markets and states, requires a constant effort to educate the public. It would remind people that any government ceases to be legitimate when it allows social inequalities to grow, ratifies the crumbling of political democracy, and accepts the subordination of national sovereignty."

Next time one of those armored money transporters passes me by, I'll try to not think about whose fortune it is that is being carted off to some unseen vault. Instead, I will take a moment to think about the driver and guard inside and whether or not they ever think of how their freight could almost immediately be put to inequality reducing uses. For families without health or dental plans, kids who go to school most mornings without lunches packed, homeless people who remain on society's outer margins, many fading away well before they reach sixty. Thinking for a moment, will of course not make the driver take a wrong turn. However, those with the safe boxes and access to the underground vaults are the ones we should all be thinking about, as they try to stay out of our sight while having their Government allies, keep electronic eyes and ears on us.

---

[i] When trying to access the report online on 1 June, the link did not open regrettably.
http://www.npaid.org/content/search?SearchText=inequality

[ii] 'Divided We Stand: Why Inequality Keeps Rising', OECD,2011
http://www.oecd.org/els/soc/49499779.pdf

Note that the "Why' presented in the report is surely debatable!

[iii]

ILO, 2012: "Global Wage Report 2012/13: Wages and Equitable Growth"
Also has an informative 2 minute Youtube clip on the report.
http://www.ilo.org/global/research/global-reports/global-wage-report/2012/lang--en/index.htm

[iv] EUROSTAT – Youth Unemployment 2012Q4
http://epp.eurostat.ec.europa.eu/statistics_explained/index.php?title=File:Youth_unemployment,_2012Q4_(%25).png&filetimestamp=201304
18091546

[v]

http://www.ids.ac.uk/news/risky-jobs-hunger-rations-and-domestic-violence-new-ids-research-reveals-the-hidden-social-costs-of-today-s-high-food-prices

Crumbs of capitalism for you and me

Glenn Brigaldino, © 2013

Newtopia-Link: http://newtopiamagazine.wordpress.com/2013/01/15/crumbs-of-capitalism-for-you-and-me

Our ruling class steers us into disaster after disaster, cheering for ruinous wars... But accountability, it seems, is something that applies only to people at the bottom....

Thomas Frank, Easy Chair, in:

Harper's, August 2012

The platitudes are not new. Only nowadays, they ring hollower than ever before: 'We are living above our means', 'When times are hard we all have to make sacrifices' or 'First things will get worse before they can get any better'. What was initially described as the financial crisis of 2008/09 is now described on Wikipedia as the '2007–2012 global financial crisis' (1) And what a crisis it is turning out to be, already half a decade long and with no end in sight. The Governments in rich and poor countries alike have struggled to contain the crisis but their policy fixes have done little to tackle the causes which are largely rooted in an intensified economic globalization that increasingly eludes attempts at political regulation or democratic accountability.

In 2010 protestors around the world joined 'Occupy Now!' campaigns, to voice their discontent and take political action to oppose the injustices and inequalities of the globalised capitalist system. In the USA it is election year and 'the economy' will be the 'front & centre' topic debated in the popular media. What the Occupy movement has highlighted, that rather than smart-talk and pseudo science about which economic models and strategies can 'turn things around' the real question to ask is 'who's' economy are we talking about?

This is essentially what is meant by 'political economy': what is an economic system based upon, how is it organized, who are the people controlling the economic system and what social forces exist or can be politically mobilized to ensure economic decisions benefit all of society and mot disproportionally a few of its privileged members.

Truly a taller order to discuss than the polished and intellectually limited debates that usually find their way into the broadcast superficial debates and the pretty charts that pass as analysis that are produced by the opinion pollsters.

Many of our mainstreamed TV commentators were quick to voice outcries of injustice when the French national assembly voted to tax the highest earners in the country at a rate of 75 per cent, following on a campaign promise made by recently elected President Francois Hollande.

The measure would affect earnings of more than €1 million ($1.27 million) per year but only for the next two years. It would be paid by an estimated 1500 people and provide the government with an extra €210 million ($267 million) in revenue per year.[v] If such an amount were made available in the US, it would be sufficient, assuming a lower-end average estimate of $750 a month, to cover daycare for over 350 000 children. That this any kids and many more do not have the chance to go to day care does not stir up any outcry from the aforementioned commentators.[v]

The financial crisis cannot be meaningfully discussed or properly understood without situating the finance dimension of the economy into the much broader, systemic crisis of the global development model we have come to view as 'globalization'. A positive side-effect of the increased attention to the turmoil in global markets is the heightened awareness of economic in equalities and injustices throughout the world.

In the homeland of un-controlled capitalism, the numbers have been lop-sided for decades. In short:

> "In the United States, wealth is highly concentrated in a relatively few hands. As of 2007, the top 1% of households (the upper class) owned 34.6% of all privately held wealth, and the next 19% (the managerial, professional, and small business stratum) had 50.5%, which means that just 20% of the people owned a remarkable 85%, leaving only 15% of the wealth for the bottom 80% (wage and salary workers)." (2)

As the crisis persists, governments become deeply dependent on the very financial institutions which have fed the global debt crisis with their insatiable hunger for ever-rising profits.

Around the world we seem to be witnessing " ...the drama of democratic states being turned into debt-collecting agencies on behalf of a global oligarchy of investors", as

> ".. the markets' have begun to dictate in unprecedented ways what presumably sovereign and democratic states may still do for their citizens and what they must refuse them. The same Manhattan-based ratings agencies that were instrumental in bringing about the disaster of the global money industry are now threatening to

downgrade the bonds of states that accepted a previously unimaginable level of new debt to rescue that industry and the capitalist economy as a whole." (3)

There are solid arguments is support of reversing of wealth accumulation amongst the numerical minuscule but politically nearly untouchable ultra-rich in North America. Indeed, the arguments for radical reversal of income inequality must be made at a global scale. But while the state once also played a buffering role through redistributive and welfare programs and acknowledgement of labour rights and demands, the state today is far less of an ally of the disadvantaged than it has been in decades.

While financial bailouts are created for those who regularly push the capitalist market to near-collapse, the low-waged, seniors and unemployed are those who are expected to jump off so-called fiscal cliffs.

This pattern of state retreat from the public and civil spheres of society in favor of the corporate and privileged spheres has become a globalised, thus deepening an already significant legitimacy deficit amongst the still formally democratic but increasingly semi-representative political systems especially in the richer countries of the North.

> "… (W)ith the penetration of the market has come not a retreat of the State, but rather a shift in the State's priorities. States no longer prioritize being responsive and accountable to their populations, but rather increasingly look to protect and advance the interests of corporations and economies at the expense of society.
>
> Neoliberal globalization has, moreover, not only intensified exploitation at the workplace and extended exploitation to the sphere of social reproduction, in such matters as health care and education; it has extended its own reach to the furthest corners of the global South."[v]

However those with power and in control of society's political and economic institutions tend to be among the wealthy themselves and obviously have no interest in dismantling the towering podium they and their rich friends are comfortably sitting upon. Even as the global crisis deepens and spreads, the

> "… trend in the U.S. and Canada to rising income inequality thus leads to periodic financial crises, greater volatility of aggregate income and, as governments respond to mass unemployment with counter-cyclical fiscal policies, a compounding instability of public finances. ….. The conundrum in all this inequality-induced macro-economic instability is that it clearly can be avoided. A steeply progressive income tax system can reduce the instability implications of increasing inequality …. Yet, in both the U.S. and Canada, the progressivity of the income tax system has been

substantially eroded, over the same period in which the pre-tax incomes of the top 1% have grown most strongly. (4)

Even officially, the poverty rate for the U.S. stands at 15 percent for 2011. Poverty is greatest among children (21.9 percent), compared with seniors (8.7 percent) and working-age adults (13.7 percent)..... the median annual household income declined for the second year in a row, to $50,054 and thus, lower than it has been since 1996. ᵛ

Indeed, as Sam Pizzigati has said, 'most Americans have essentially spent the last 20 years on a go-nowhere treadmill. They're working longer and harder and have zero new wealth to show for their labor.' (5)

To elaborate a bit on the case of Canada, the arguments in favor of a more equal society were largely acted upon in the past, when universal healthcare was introduced nationally and wage earners saw wage increases above annual inflation rates.

Those days are long gone and although many Canadians still believe that 'things are better here', there are few meaningful statistics to back- up such a feel-good psyche. For years, productivity and innovation rates in Canada have been falling as wage incomes remain below those in US.

Among peers, Canada is being noticed, for all the wrong reasons:

> "Income inequality among working-age persons has been rising in Canada, particularly since the mid-1990s . .... and is above the OECD average. ... Moreover, that of the richest 0.1% more than doubled, from 2% to 5.3%. At the same time, the top federal marginal income tax rates saw a marked decline: dropping from 43% in 1981 to 29% in 2010. ... Taxes and benefits reduce inequality less in Canada than in most OECD countries. (6)

The numbers are there for anyone to read:

> "In OECD countries today, the average income of the richest 10% of the population is about nine times that of the poorest 10% – a ratio of 9 to 1. However, the ratio varies widely from one country to another. It is much lower than the OECD average in the Nordic and many continental European countries, but reaches 10 to 1 in Italy, Japan, Korea, and the United Kingdom; around 14 to 1 in Israel, Turkey, and the United States; and 27 to 1 in Mexico and Chile."

Recent OECD reports show that there is nothing inevitable about such unsettling, growing inequalities. However, being essentially a 'rich man's club' amongst the world's nations, the OECD is unable to prescribe any policies or even political strategies that could call for abandoning the free-market capitalist growth model the global rich thrive upon. Capsizing their own ship is not an option the 1% will ever contemplate.

The language of 'change' thus remains nebulous and mostly general in nature: "Globalisation and technological changes offer opportunities but also raise challenges that can be tackled with effective and well-targeted policies". As the global working classes continues to impoverish they are encourages to stay the course of free markets continuous economic shocks and downturns as somehow, the very system that unleashes these crisis, will miraculously self-correct itself.

One serious consequence of prolonged inequality that results from 'the war on salaries' is the erosion of health and life expectancy among the poorer segments of society. Simply speaking, the poor live less healthy and shorter lives than the rich.

(c) 2012, G.Brigaldino

Research published in the online journal 'Population Health Metrics' demonstrates that "during the period 2000 to 2007, life expectancy in the US and most of its counties fell behind the progress seen in other nations."

The authors go on to note that the

> "US has extremely large geographic and racial disparities, with some communities having life expectancies already well behind those of the best-performing nations.

In 2007, life expectancy at birth for American men and women was 75.6 and 80.8 years, ranking 37th and 37th, respectively, in the world. Across US counties, life expectancy at birth ranged from 65.9 to 81.1 years for men and 73.5 to 86.0 years for women. … The extent of geographic inequality is substantially larger in the US than in the UK, Canada, or Japan.

In spite of the US maintaining 'its position as the country that spent the most per capita on health care throughout this period (2000-2007)." (7)

One would expect that very few of the <1% reside in a country with a life expectancy of only 65.9 years.

From a public health perspective, it is no new phenomena that those who are poor experience dismal health outcomes. The trend is common in the world's poorest countries and regions. There, as in the homeland of inequality-breeding capitalism, the 2008 global economic crisis has had a disturbing and sad effect upon women and children.

Researchers at the Asian Development Bank have reported that

"economic downturns tend to have stronger effects, especially for girls, than economic booms: life expectancy of girls and boys increases by an estimated 2 years during good economic periods but decreases by 7 years for girls, and 6 years for boys, during adverse economic times.

There is "an average increase in infant mortality of 7.4 deaths per 1000 births for girls compared with 1.5 deaths per 1000 births for boys for every one or more unit fall in Gross Domestic Product (GDP)." (8)

That inequality has no upsides for the poor goes without saying, and those within a society who tend to benefit when inequality levels are high and entrenched, cannot deny that

"Inequality has the greatest impact on the poor and those living in the most deprived areas of society. Children do particularly badly in unequal societies – from worse infant mortality rates, through to lower levels of participation in further education. In more unequal societies, children are more likely to be overweight, to be victims of bullying, and to become teenage mothers.

Once they become adults in more unequal societies they are more likely to have mental health problems, to have problems with drugs and alcohol, to work longer hours and have more debt pressures on family life. And social mobility is lower in more unequal societies, so it is more difficult for children to escape from intergenerational cycles of poverty and deprivation."

On both accounts, with regard to inequality and child well-being, the US performs extremely dismal compared to other rich countries. (9)

This trend is threatening to become turn into a common pattern in rich(er) and poor(er) countries alike, as being 'born unequal' is clearly related to worrisome disparities in health outcomes.

For example,

"... disparities in health outcomes do not only exist in poorer countries. In Canada, one of the world's eight richest countries (characterised by deep regional inequalities, with child poverty rates varying from just over 10% to more than twice that), low-income children are 2.5 times more likely to have a problem with vision, hearing, speech or mobility."[v]

So while the effects of inequality are there for all to see, pro-market Governments are finding it hard to take off their sunglasses. The platitudes heralded from G8 and G20 summits alike, capture little attention among the working poor and unemployed. First subtle advice to reverse course is now even emerging from within the summiteers' very own policy think tank, namely the OECD.

Perhaps somewhat daringly for a mainstream organization, it has sub-titled a recent publication 'The Role of Empowerment'.

On the cover of the 300-page report, a chain bursts apart, presumably to demonstrate a bold move for "strengthening poor people's organizations, providing them with more control over assets".

The report goes on to observe:

"Globally, extreme and persistent inequalities linked to poverty, gender, ethnicity and language are holding back the development of human capabilities. Policies that successfully counteract such inequalities include improving accessibility and affordability by cutting fees and informal charges; improving quality by providing highly skilled teachers and health workers; expanding entitlements and opportunities by integrating health and education strategies into wider anti-marginalization policies, such as social protection; reinforcing legal entitlements; and supporting a fairer distribution of public spending. "(10)

Word has gotten out earlier still, as few illusions exist among the authors of a 2011 ILO report spell out who question the effectiveness and indeed, the economic relevant of the so-called recovery programs launched so far.

As they point out:

> "The global economic outlook has deteriorated significantly since 2010, signaling that the policies implemented to date have failed on a number of fronts. ... As long-term unemployment rises and workers begin to leave the labour market entirely, the window for taking decisive action is closing. Urgent action to place employment creation at the centre of the recovery plan is necessary. "(11)

Such doubts are echoed by UNICEF, which notes that

> "...ironically, while fiscal stimulus packages mainly benefited wealthier income groups—not the poor—during the first phase of the crisis, budget cuts are disproportionately impacting the poor during the second phase." (12)

The arguments and statistical evidence demonstrating 'failure by design' of what is still called the free market, is substantial. Only protagonists of the status quo, those who either indentify with the 1% or belong to them (or both), put on a serious face when defending their 'more of the same' economic medicine, or their phony potions for economic recovery.

The math is actually quite simple: what the wealthy are given in tax breaks essentially corresponds to wage erosion, limiting of labor benefits and cuts in public services to the unwealthy. In the past year we have all witnessed what has happened in Greece and is now being replicated in Spain, where on top of massive job and income losses, about half of all youth and young workers are now unemployed.

Basically,

"while governments across Europe are making cuts in public expenditure to reduce their deficits, the moral case for proper tax enforcement is particularly strong: every €1,000 of tax that the rich avoid paying creates the need for another €1,000 of cuts to services to the least well off.

There is an awful inevitability about how the poorest end up paying for the mistakes and dishonesty of the rich whose actions led to the present recession. The scale of tax avoidance among the rich almost begs everyone else to go on a tax strike until the rich are made to pay." (13)

Maintaining profits for the rich remains the unarticulated mantra of the political class as they continue to preach restraint to the masses. The 'we all need to tighten our belts' rhetoric may have subsided under conditions of increasingly blatant inequality as this kind of hollow talk angers more than it consoles. There are more subtle ways and almost comically creative ones when it comes to squeezing more money out of those who are already living from pay cheque to pay cheque. We probably have all realized that food prices in the supermarket have risen.

The ways in which higher prices are passed on are intended to keep consumers in spending mood. New carton designs for your favorite cereal chase the fact that there can be 10 to 15% less cereal inside the box but the price is the same as before.

At the ever-bustling Dollar-stores, what used to be had for a buck now costs $1.25. Basically everywhere else, products displayed as 'On Sale', are nowadays often sold at what used to be the regular price, but are shown as 'normally' having a 20% higher regular price. Many other products now come in smaller packaging while the aisle price is unchanged, creating the illusion of 'stable prices'. Last year a friend of mine bought red bricks for a backyard footpath. When he bought more of them this year to extend the path, he discovered that although the price was unchanged, the bricks were now 2cm shorter.

At school, kids learn nothing of political economy. Instead they are fed half-truths and economic fairytales of how growth produces jobs, told that honest work pays or are led to believe that the 'laws of supply and demand' somehow miraculously determine prices in what is still labeled as a 'free market'.

Our youth are encouraged to accept student loan and credit card debt to drown in: they will be enticed to consume their lives away and buy things that often only meet artificially generated needs and to burden themselves with mortgages until they have retirement in sight. Their kids will hopefully do much of the same it is hoped by the 'business world', in order to keep the lopsided consumer society afloat a little longer.

The notion that everybody pays taxes for public goods and services has turned into little more than a mirage. In fact the richer you are, the less you pay anything that resembles a 'fair share'. Share-issuing companies have adhered to this principle for decades, knowing that if they shift their profits to subsidiaries, frequently based in tax havens, and apply accounting techniques that allow them to demonstrate an annual loss year after year, their tax 'burden' will be zero.

Especially in the US, the 'don't raise taxes' rhetoric is nothing else but the rallying call of the ultra-rich to avoid paying taxes at the rate an average Wal-Mart employee has to pay. Such favourism comes with a hefty price tag for the poor, in terms of declining incomes and reduced or eroding public services:

> "The share of the federal budget funded by corporate income taxes has dropped dramatically since the 1940s, from 28.8 percent of the budget to 10.3 percent.

In 2010, U.S. corporations avoided approximately $60 billion in U.S. corporate income taxes by using a variety of devices and gimmicks to shift profits to foreign subsidiaries, while the Fortune 100 companies received some $89.6 billion in federal contracts. … major U.S, corporations are avoiding tens of billions of dollars in U.S. corporate income taxes through a variety of devices and gimmicks which allow them to hide profits overseas, often artificially assigning these profits to countries with little or no corporate income tax. (14)

So one can confidently say that the numbers are in, the data is confirmed and the system-discrediting evidence has been produced: inequality is deep and widespread, increasing and worst of all, it is depriving millions of people around the world of decent livelihoods and of hope. Any society that idly stands by or turns a cold shoulder to the politics and economics that create massive inequality is arguably an unethical one. "What to do about it" is a question any decent person will be asking.

Once this is asked, the central issue of how to change society arises and importantly, the "who" will do something about it needs to be asked. The search for the progressive 'historical subject' is on.

In his well written book, 'The Great Divergence' Tim Noah has addressed many of the inequality concerns also expressed in this article. Disappointingly, the final chapter titled "What We Can Do About It" falls short and does not say who the "we" actually are or to convincingly elaborate on any "how" to overcome today's global inequality. (15)

Ultimately, Noah places hope in benign reforms and technocratic fixes of the system and in those who have historically perpetuated it. He seems at a loss to locate a social counterforce to the ruling economic and political class. Rightfully so, he recognizes the changed frame of mind amongst those who are upset about growing injustices.

Where once anger turned into at times violent political protest and revolt, today, resentment is said to dominate and is often kept inside. I suggest that this might be true for many people; the emergence of the Occupy movement has opened up a multitude of possibilities to oppose, challenge, bypass and undermine the inequality economy. (16)

It is too early to say that the Occupy protests are merely a flare-up of dissent but I would wager that although the movements' intensity and visibility might heavily fluctuate, the desire and preparedness to engage in lasting socioeconomic change is genuine and is bound to have a prolonged, dislodging impact upon the current capitalist political economy.

The people who oppose, object and revolt against the capitalist world of systematic inequality, are of course those posing a serious challenge to capitalism and its' 'business as usual', technocratic and cosmetic approach to dealing not only with economic, but with social and environmental issues as well. It is quite possible that the more radically they (the Occupy movement and its supporters) question and act against the system, the greater their revolutionary impact potentially becomes: within the core capitalist countries and throughout the emerging alternative centers as well as on the economic margins and desolate geographic fringes of what has also been labeled 'armed globalization'.

The ruling classes within free-market preaching states may increasingly fail to compensate for the market failures and environmental and social consequences of unrestrained capitalism. It comes as no surprise that the global governing elites

"..offer only a technical fix to the present (systemic) crisis and have no real…intention of conducting any meaningful radical reform or transformation of the system itself."

But precisely such transformation is needed and is most likely, if indeed at all in the nearer future, to be brought about by

".. all those very people who have been negatively affected by the present system and who, through their lived experiences, realize the need for radical thinking and for radical action" (17)

As 'forces of resistance', these people are likely to continue to form alliances and organize through social networks, and engage in 'conscious collective political action' that challenge the ruling system and unjust distribution of wealth, opportunities and political power. What is fascinating is that with the mobilization of protest and dissent in the Occupy / We are the 99% - movement, indeed such new forms of organizing protest and political action have emerged, facilitated notably through social media (the political outcomes of such mobilization in the wake of the 'Arab Spring', have yet to demonstrate how profoundly they are rooted and based on democratic and socially inclusive aspirations and principles).

In North America and Europe, it has taken many by surprise that a protest movement can in fact be distinctly leaderless: thus representing a stark organizational contrast and alternative to the system-conform efforts of the so-called leaders of our existing, nation states. It is a protest movement, as we have witnessed in Quebec where students have vehemently opposed tuition hikes, which is prepared to ask questions that simply are not asked in the mainstreamed media, such as

> "Democracy, as viewed by the other side, is tagged as 'representative' – and we wonder just what it represents." (18)

Spontaneous actions of people who've 'had enough' of being ripped off, of being manipulated by entertainment and consumer industries, or being taken advantage of from the 'cradle to the grave', are finding new ways to express their dissent. As violent conflicts rage outside the borders of our core 'homeland' capitalist countries, living inside the 'free world' has lost much of its meaning for many. The inequalities in the 'land(s) of the free' have definitely become synonymous with 'pursuit of happiness' for those living the good life while floating on their wonderful clouds of luxury, while below, it never stops raining injustices on us common mortals.

References

(1) Wikipedia, 2007–2012 global financial crisis, http://en.wikipedia.org/wiki/Financial_crisis_of_2007%E2%80%932010

(2) Distribution of net worth and financial wealth in the United States, 1983-2007 by G. William Domhoff: http://www2.ucsc.edu/whorulesamerica/power/wealth.html

(3) THE CRISES OF DEMOCRATIC CAPITALISM, Wolfgang Streeck in: New Left Review 71 Sept/Oct 2011

(4) Instability Implications of Increasing Inequality - What can be learned from North America?, Lars Osberg, 2012 **http://www.policyalternatives.ca/publications/reports/instability-implications-increasing-inequality**

Also see: Of the 1%, by the 1%, for the 1%, Joseph E. Stiglitz, 2011 http://www.vanityfair.com/society/features/2011/05/top-one-percent-201105#

(5) Sam Pizzigati, Magic Act: Making the Super Rich Disappear, June 2012 'Too Much' commentary of the project of the Program on Inequality and the Common Good of the D.C.-based Institute for Policy Studies, http://toomuchonline.org/magic-act-making-the-super-rich-disappear

Also see: The war on salaries - Enough is enough by Sam Pizzigati in Le Monde diplomatique Feb 2012 "US radicals came up a century ago with sound proposals for a maximum income, enforced through progressive taxation, to ensure that the rich couldn't so easily buy political influence, as well as to adjust inequality ".

(6) Divided We Stand - Why Inequality Keeps Rising, OECD 2011 http://www.oecd.org/document/51/0,3746,en_2649_33933_49147827_1_1_1_1,00.html

In terms of living standards, it has recently been reported that since 1981, "Canadians experienced a widening of income and wealth inequalities. There have been poverty reductions, but the reductions were not nearly as large as the increase in wealth inequality.

See:

Center for the Study of Living Standards, Research Report 2011-17, Andrew Sharpe and Christopher Ross
http://ideas.repec.org/p/sls/resrep/1117.html

(7) Falling behind: life expectancy in US counties from 2000 to 2007 in an international context
Sandeep C Kulkarni, Alison Levin-Rector, Majid Ezzati and Christopher JL Murray Kulkarni et al. Population Health Metrics 2011, 9:16 http://www.pophealthmetrics.com/content/9/1/16

(8) The other crisis: the economics and financing of maternal, newborn and child health in Asia, Ian Anderson, Henrik Axelson, and B-K Tan, in: In *Health Policy and Planning, 2010*

http://heapol.oxfordjournals.org/content/26/4/288.long

(9) The Spirit Level: Why Greater Equality Makes Societies Stronger , Bill Kerry, Kate E. Pickett and Richard Wilkinson, in:

Child Poverty and Inequality: New Perspectives, Isabel Ortiz, Louise Moreira Daniels, Sólrún Engilbertsdóttir (Eds), UNICEF, 2012 http://www.unicef.org/socialpolicy/index_62108.html

(10) OECD (2012), Poverty Reduction and Pro-Poor Growth: The Role of Empowerment;
http://dx.doi.org/10.1787/9789264168350-en

(11) World of work report 2011: Making markets work for jobs / International Labour Office. 2011

http://www.ilo.org/global/publications/ilo-bookstore/order-online/books/WCMS_166021/lang--en/index.htm

(12) United Nations Children's Fund (UNICEF), 2012, A Recovery for All: Rethinking Socio-Economic Policies for Children and Poor Households, Isabel Ortiz and Matthew Cummins (Editors)

"An analysis of the winners and losers of the crisis must further consider that, particularly in the economies of the Organisation for Economic Cooperation and Development (OECD), a large share of stimulus packages included tax cuts, mainly through reductions in personal income tax for the wealthy. Thus, ironically, while fiscal stimulus packages mainly benefited wealthier income groups—not the poor—during the first phase of the crisis, budget cuts are disproportionately impacting the poor during the second phase.

The massive bailouts for the financial industry further indicate that the real problem in addressing this global crisis was not the availability of money, but rather the lack of political will. In fact, the amount of money needed annually to achieve the MDGs is a miniscule fraction of the estimated trillions of public money that was mobilized for bank bailouts."
http://www.unicef.org/socialpolicy/index_62107.html

(13) Richard Wilkinson & Kate Pickett in: TAX JUSTICE FOCUS - THE INEQUALITY EDITION THIRD, 2012, issue 2, downloaded from: http://www.newleftproject.org

(14) Corporate America. Untaxed. Tax Avoidance on the Rise. Samuel Kang and Tuan Ngo

http://greenlining.org/resources/pdfs/CorporateAmericaUntaxed.pdf

(15) The Great Divergence: America's Growing Inequality Crisis and What We Can Do about It, Timothy Noah, 2012; Reviewed by Felix Salmon in New York Times:

http://www.mercurynews.com/entertainment/ci_20894263/review-books-from-paul-krugman-and-timothy-noah?source=rss

(16) For an interview Michael Hardt, co-Author of Empire and *Multitude see: Democracy on the Defensive – September/October 2005 issue of Newtopia Magazine, interview conducted by Glenn Brigaldino.*

http://newtopiamagazine.wordpress.com/2012/03/09/archives-democracy-on-the-defensive-interview-with-michael-hardt-co-author-of-empire-and-multitude

(17) Going South: capitalist crisis, systemic crisis, civilisational crisis, Barry Gills in Third World Quarterly: vol. 31, no. 2, pp. 169-184, 2010

This article argues that the current protracted and severe financial and economic crisis is only one aspect of a larger multidimensional set of simultaneous and interacting crises on a global scale. The article constructs an overarching framework of analysis of this unique conjecture of global crises. The three principal crisis aspects are: an economic crisis of (over) accumulation of capital; a world systemic crisis (which includes a global centre-shift in the locus of production, growth and capital accumulation), and a hegemonic transition (which implies long term changes in global governance structures and institutions); and a worldwide civilisational crisis, situated in the socio-historical structure itself, encompassing a comprehensive environmental crisis and the consequences of a lack of correspondence and coherence in the material and ideational structures of world order. In these ways, the global system is now `going south'.

All three main aspects of the global crisis provoke and require commensurate radical social and political responses and self-protective measures, not only to restore systemic stability but to transform the world system.

http://www.tandfonline.com/doi/abs/10.1080/01436591003711926

In "Days of Destruction, Days of Revolt" (Knopf, 2012) Chris Hedges and Joe Sacco show in words and drawings what life looks like in places where the marketplace rules without constraints, where human beings and the natural world are used and then discarded to maximize profit. For an upbeat review see Tim Knight at:

http://www.zerohedge.com/contributed/2012-08-05/days-destruction-days-revolt

(18) Share our future – the CLASSE manifesto, reposted by www.OccupyWallSt.org July 14, 2012. The document goes on to note:

This brand of « democracy » comes up for air once every four years, for a game of musical chairs. While elections come and go, decisions remain unchanged, serving the same interests: those of leaders who prefer the murmurs of lobbyists to the clanging of pots and pans.

Each time the people raises its voice in discontent, on comes the answer: emergency laws, with riot sticks, pepper spray, tear gas. When the elite feels threatened, no principle is sacred, not even those principles they preach: for them, democracy works only when we, the people keep our mouths shut.

http://occupywallst.org/article/share-our-future-classe-manifesto

We are the Experts and the Economy belongs to the Working Class

A cross-Atlantic, online 'Armchair' conversation with Professor John Weeks

Interview by Glenn Brigaldino, Newtopia Associate © 2013

Newtopia-Link:

http://newtopiamagazine.wordpress.com/2013/09/15/we-are-the-experts-and-the-economy-belongs-to-the-working-class

John Weeks (JW) is professor emeritus at the School of Oriental and African Studies in London, U.K. As a critical economist and commentator, he has widely explored and analyzed the inner workings of a capitalist system running amok with the lives of the working class – from Sierra Leone to the shores and homelands of the US Empire.

Newtopia associate Glenn Brigaldino (GB) has virtually sat down with Prof. Weeks, to discuss some inner workings and traits of our economic system and how it might be saved, from itself and the 1%.

© 2011, G.Brigaldino

(GB): Since the 2008/9 global economic upheaval, recovery has been slow, spotty and in particular for the working classes anemic or non-existent. Banks, mortgage brokers and the car manufacturers along with the oil industry, weathered the self-induced storm fairly well. The governments of the major capitalist economies turned socialist and 'bailed the culprits out while letting their working citizens foot the bill. Today, the storm has certainly calmed down from the turbulences of five years ago, but a massive, accelerated redistribution of wealth from the bottom to the top 0.1% of society has been the price to pay.

In some 'developed' economies, notably in the Eurozone, unemployment rates have hit and even surpassed 20% in some countries, especially young people are heavily affected and face uncertain futures. My question to you Prof. Weeks:

In principle, growth fixated capitalist societies are capable of achieving annual growth rates of 2% or 3%, distribution issues aside. Does this mean that it will take 10 or 15 years to erase double digit unemployment rates or, can the globalised free-market system 'deliver' full employment before 2020, at least in the Eurozone, Japan and North America, the traditional capitalist countries?

(JW): If "austerity" policies continue in Europe and Obama yields to conservative pressures to reduce public spending in the United States, no substantial recovery can occur. By "substantial" I mean two percent or above. In the absence of an active fiscal policy private investment will remain depressed, reinforcing the public expenditure cuts. With the major capitalist countries trapped in self-imposed stagnation we cannot expect any substantial demand stimulus from exports.

This does not mean zero growth, because the nature of capitalist economies is to expand. However, it will be very slow at best. Should policy change and governments use fiscal policy to stimulate growth, rapid expansion could occur in the early years of the recovery, on the basis of idle labor (unemployment) and idle capacity. With conscious, purposeful fiscal policy the recovery could begin quite rapidly, as was the case in the first year of the Obama fiscal stimulus of 2009, though that stimulus was well below what was necessary to achieve sustained growth.

In the longer term the growth rate of the developed capitalist economies would level off, determined by the rate of growth of productivity. Investment, low in almost all of the developed countries for the last decade, could raise productivity growth. The experience of the 1950s and 1960s indicates that developed countries have the potential to sustain growth rates close of four percent per annum.

So to give you a number, full employment anytime soon, in less than 10 years without considerable economic policy shifts, is not possible.

(GB): In the early 1970s, a group of social and economic experts associated with the 'Club of Rome' think tank published a critical and forward-looking report titled 'The Limits of Growth". If I can capture the central argument in a few words, it was postulated that the earth's natural resources are finite and unrestrained and accelerated growth in consumption and profit driven economies is not only unsustainable, it can also not be replicated on a global scale. A dramatic reconfiguration and rethink of the dominant capitalist development model is called for.

Since then, it seems there have been very few limits to economic growth. Globalization has taken off some 15 years ago: best exemplified by the economic rise of China which since then has possibly grown to a greater extent than the GDP of all of Europe in 1972.

Has the earth's carrying capacity been grossly under-estimated and have technology and innovation opened the door to a long-term period of efficient management of ecological challenges without the need for drastic changes to the institutions and social relationships within capitalist free-market economies?

(JW): I am not an expert on the relationship between the environment and the economy. However, I would make a few general points. It is in the nature of capital to attempt to expand without limit. Therefore, unregulated capitalism can and may destroy our environment beyond repair. Whether there is a regulated form of capitalism that would not destroy the environment is an extremely controversial and complex issue.

Production processes within capitalist relations that are consistent with safeguarding the environment might provide the investment opportunities to drive sustained growth.

Extremely strict public sector regulation would be required in accord with a clear political goal to drastically reduce and ultimately, eliminate the use of hydrocarbon fuels and to drop all nuclear options.

(GB): Whenever I spend a few days in the United States, just an hours' drive from where I live up north, the contrast between affluence and living beyond the outer margins of economic well-being, strike me as extremely pronounced. Usually I visit upstate New York, where nature is at its scenic best. You can genuinely appreciate the environment, especially In the Adirondack region. At the same time, you'll find it hard to ignore the countless crumbling, paint-starved houses, almost entire towns in places. Most people living there are likely to have only modestly paid jobs, but will still almost all have a vehicle or two, some maybe even a small motorboat.

Many will own sizeable arrays of aged furnishings and rarely utilized household items, accumulated over the years of living in the world's largest consumer society. While passing through the towns and small cities, you will sense that many local residents may spend more time shopping and in fast food outlets, than engage in outdoor activities or with direct social interactions with fellow local citizens. Maybe not and I guess you are wondering by now, "is there any question coming?"

(JW): I'm sure there is!

(GB): Alright, here it is: would you contest the thesis that after generations of actual and imagined material affluence, even as real impoverishment among citizens in affluent countries deepens, that the large majority of people in these European and North American countries would rather go on a free shopping spree and keep on consuming as if there is no tomorrow than occupy a shopping mall to protest low wages and unfair prices?

(JW): I disagree with the "shopping spree" thesis. Most people who go "shopping" in the developed countries are poor or near-poor, lower and lower-middle class. These people are "shopping" to house, clothe and feed their families. To do so in the United States, households have gone massively into debt, a phenomenon closely linked to the decline in real wages.

To demonstrate this, I provide a box from my forthcoming book, *The Economics of the 1%.* It demonstrates that most US households have responded to stagnant incomes by the only way they can, borrowing.

At the 1936 Democratic convention, Franklin Roosevelt said in his acceptance speech,

> "The hours men and women worked, the wages they received, the conditions of their labor — these had passed beyond the control of the people, and were imposed by this new industrial dictatorship."

Now, in the 21st century, we have a re-invigorated industrial and financial dictatorship

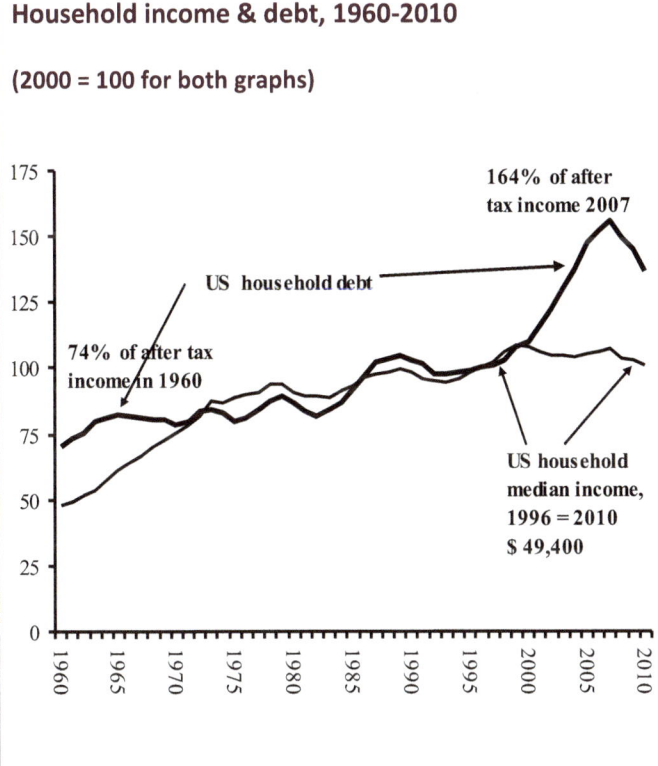

Household income & debt, 1960-2010

(2000 = 100 for both graphs)

164% of after tax income 2007

US household debt

74% of after tax income in 1960

US household median income, 1996 = 2010 $ 49,400

Note: Household debt is measured as its ratio to household income.

Source: Economic Report of the President 2011

- During the second half of the 20th century US households had relatively low indebtedness. From the end of WWII into the 1980s the ratio of household debt to income fluctuated in the 70-80 percent range. In the 1980s Congress deregulated the financial sector to allow people to borrow on the value of their homes.

- This "benefit" of financial deregulation coincided with stagnation of household income and rapidly rising indebtedness. The combination was no accident. The rising debt indicates that most households struggled to maintain living standards as income stagnated.

- Making that struggle more difficult were falling real wages, offset by more income earners, typically through more women in paid work.

- Lower pay, stagnant income and accumulating debt, consumer sovereignty in action.

(GB): Thanks for sharing this preview, I just wonder what this table would look like if poverty rates were superimposed onto the table: would it show that while the actual number of people in poverty might have risen, the percentage portion of the overall population they make up, may have dropped – could that be?

(JW): I have a similar diagram for poverty rates, which shows that the share of the population in poverty did not decline in the 2000s and rose substantially during 2008-2011, to about 15-16% of households.

(GB): Prof. Weeks, any thoughts on the ongoing civil strife and violent political turmoil in Syria and Egypt? There could be good reason to believe, that democratic aspirations do not have much of a chance at materializing in societies seemingly caught in 'time warps' of cultural and theological conservatism. Democratic civil societies throughout the 'Arab spring" world are at best in their infancy. Most certainly they are marred by ideological conflicts that oscillate between secular democratic society and theocracy. Many of the social norms and values held by large parts of the population, may well be diametrically opposed to integration into the free-market driven, profit oriented globalised economic (dis-)order.

Do you see concrete options to arrive at peaceful political settlements that all factions can agree to in order to (re-) build democratic social institutions and provide economic opportunities to ensure the needs of rapidly growing populations can be met in a sustainable manner?

(JW): I lack the expertise to provide any useful insight into events in North Africa and the Middle East. I would only make the general comment that these events of the last five to ten years clearly demonstrate a marked decline of US influence in the region. The US government no longer exerts dominant control in the region, not even in Israel where the far-Right government has repeatedly treated the Obama administration with the contempt it so richly deserves. A rare bit of optimism came with the recent refusal of the UK Parliament to endorse military action in Syria. For reasons of past experience rather than current expertise, I strongly believe that US and European intervention would make conditions worse for the Syrian people.

(GB): As we discuss this issue, we can almost assume with certainty, that the US will have launched some sort of attack on the regime in Damascus by the time this Newtopia interview goes online or shortly thereafter. As for matters having, if not gotten worse, then at least not any better than prior to an US-driven invasion, we only need to take note of the resurfacing sectarian violence in Iraq, where over 1000 people have been killed in July alone.

(JW): Also, recall that the US government has killed hundreds of civilians with drones in Afghanistan, Pakistan and elsewhere, casting the US commitment to "humanitarian intervention" into doubt.

(GB): I hope the interview questions so far have not place too much of a political spotlight on you as an expert on the inner workings of the capitalist economic system. Perhaps, with a 'closer to home' question you could offer some economic 'food-for-thought' for Newtopia's readers on how to make the economy work for them instead of mainly for the One-Percent. We all must make daily living within the confines of the inequality generating economic system we live under to keep ourselves and our loved ones 'above water'. In your opinion, are there specific actions we can take social relations to nurture or ways of living to embrace, which can ease the way we secure our livelihoods? To add on, could this be done in unison with actions to reverse political corruption, social erosion and income inequality?

(JW): I have written extensively on these issues. My clearest statement is at the end of my forthcoming book, which I provide below:

>   ***'Implementing Economics for the 99%'***

At the level of the entire economy the public sector should function as the social institution responsible for maintaining full employment, so that very one who wants a job can find one.

A government that fails in this task qualifies for Roosevelt's description of Republican administrations during 1920-1932:

"For twelve years this Nation was afflicted with hear-nothing, see-nothing, do-nothing Government. Powerful influences strive today to restore that kind of government with its doctrine that that government is best which is most indifferent."
[**Franklin D. Roosevelt** in a speech on October 31, 1936 at Madison Square Garden, New York City]

Exactly this type of government held sway in most of the advanced countries at the end of the twentieth century and into the twenty-first, whatever the political parties in power called themselves.

In essence, public sector policies were design to launch public sector increases in its expenditure to achieve a level of aggregate spending that reduced unemployment to its practical minimum. As the economy recovered, the public sector scaled back its spending to match the private sector increases. The policy package is technically simple, easily implemented and as feasible in the twenty-first century as during the immediate post World War II decades of the twentieth century.

(GB): If simple, then why don't governments in crisis today apply this approach?

(JW): Well, a fully employed work force with a large portion receiving wages inadequate to meet basic human and social needs does not serve the interest of the vast majority of working people. On the contrary, a low-wage, fully employed labor force might better meet the interests of the 1% than the scandal of the highest unemployment levels in the advanced countries since the Great Recession of the late 1920s.

A society whose economic institutions function for the many, not the few, requires the public sector to design and implement policies for an equitable distribution of income with no person and no household below the poverty line.

(GB): A social and economic issue raised just recently by fast food industry workers on strike across the US, asking for a wage increase to $15 an hour and the right to unionize.

(JW): Precisely, these are people who often have never in their entire working lives moved even an inch above the poverty line. You see, first and foremost, poverty *reduction* differs fundamentally from poverty *alleviation.* The latter involves reducing ("alleviating") the misery of the poor, while the former seeks to eliminate poverty itself.

The US "food stamp" program, later named the Electronic Benefit Transfer, which provides people with the means to purchase food and non-alcoholic drinks in supermarkets and fast food outlets, falls into the "alleviation" category. The British system of housing benefit also fits this category. At least two characteristics of these programs identify them as "alleviating":

   1) they were income ("means") tested, so only those defined as poor receive them, and

   2) they do not directly enhance the income earning potential of the recipient.

Successful poverty reduction programs enhance earning capacity and protect people against falling into poverty once out of it. For neoliberals education serves as the most important, sometimes their only, poverty reduction mechanism. While educating people to enhance skills should occur in any decent society, it does not in itself reduce poverty. The newly skilled person must find a job with take-home pay above the poverty level, as well as enjoy protection against difficulties large and small that would provoke a return to destitution.

Improving people's education may contribute substantially to poverty reduction if a society that provides health care for all, ensures a living wage, and adequately supports workers when they fall into unemployment. Without full employment, a national health system, minimum wages and unemployment protection, more education only results in more highly skilled population in poverty.

(GB): A trend increasingly observed in North America is that the costs for post-secondary education have sky-rocketed and scores of students find themselves not only in heavy debt after graduation, but also without education-relevant jobs for years, or can get into jobs that just a decade ago, required only, say a high school degree instead of a bachelors degree.

(JW): It's a trend not limited to the US and Canada, it is very real in Europe too. Not to forget that in the 'new economic power houses' like Brazil and China, there are tens of millions of graduates eagerly looking for 'at level' jobs as well, displacing youth with lower academic credentials as they move into the workforce.

(GB): An important observation to make, John. Don't experts have something to say about all of this?

(JW): There are countless shortfalls in competence among mainstream economists, the proponents of 'fakeconomics' against the welfare of society as I have come to describe them. Among its worst obfuscations for the future of humanity is the mis-treatment and mis-representation of the gathering environmental disaster.

(GB): I would be quick to add that many of the so-called fiscal experts and corporate managers themselves seem to lack basic academic skills, explaining in part how it came to happen that they tossed the global economy into the deepest turmoil we have experienced, at least in most of our lifetimes.

(JW): That is a valid point to make. Moreover, when it comes to the environment, mainstream economists, usually compare the cost of restrictions to protect our planet against the benefits of those restrictions. Many books are devoted to demonstrating how this approach misleads and misinforms decision making in general. For the environment this so-called cost-benefit approach is completely inappropriate and pernicious.

"Cost-benefit" claims to calculate the "trade off" between costs and benefits on the assumption that these apply to the entire range of possible outcomes. For the process of environmental change this approach contradicts scientific analysis and evidence on environmental change. For our climate, oceans and quality of the air itself, changes are not "marginal": they do not respond well at all to "more of the same".

Economists installed in the political and economic institutions of capitalism, provide little technical expertise for the protection of a sustainable environment. The same applies to those economists advising on the allocation of resources for different elements of health care, social welfare, labour benefits and of course education systems. In a genuinely democratic and decent society, allocation of these human necessities requires impartial and socially aware technical expertise to inform both the public and its political representatives in making these decisions.

Think of it this way: when we are sick, we consult doctors about medical care; we do not expect them to advise us on the not management of the economy. When it comes to democratic political institutions and public policies, why would we rely on unelected economic technocrats to decide who gets a decent education, which families qualify for better social benefits or who needs to be paid a decent living wage?

(GB): Before we wrap up this interview with you Prof. Weeks, I will make one more push to get some advice from you, acknowledging that your expertise may not fully extend into this field, but how do you think the political struggle for more economic justice will unfold and organize in the next two or three years? Can we hope to see the 99% gain some economic, social and political ground?

(JW): If ground is gained it will be on the basis of a rejuvenated workers' movement, through reform of existing trade unions or emergence of new ones. My son is a trade union organizer in Britain and it is the type of work he does on the stop floor and in the streets, confronting capital that brings me hope. The linking of the workers' movement to the struggle against racism and sexism represents the path to replace the capitalism of the 1% with a social democracy of the 99%.

(GB): Professor Weeks, thank you for this cross-Atlantic interview. Newtopia readers will certainly appreciate your views and insights and hopefully, share them widely both on- and offline!

(JW): I thank you for this opportunity to join in the extremely important work that you do in fostering progressive thought and action.

John Weeks has a new book forthcoming in October, 'The Economics of the 1%: How mainstream economics serves the rich, obscures reality and distorts policy', to be published by Anthem Press. You can download an information sheet on Prof. Week's web-site at http://jweeks.org

Two un-published 'Letters to the Editor' of Harper's (http://harpers.org)

(A)

For a self-proclaimed 'Anti-Economist', Jeff Madrick lavishes plenty of praise upon mainstreamed economists (A bit of good news, April). To rehash the economic myth that quantitative growth equates to more jobs and economic recovery, sounds rather illusionary and appears oddly out of place. Such myth does not acquire reputability merely because Harvard and Goldman Sachs economists subscribe to it. Few, if any political economists or Wall Street Occupiers will be impressed to find out that the House majority leader has 'twittered' this kind of news. That a Chinese manufacturing giant feels so inclined to 'allow' it's low wage workers the right to unionize, inspires contempt for the firm rather than any sort of admiration.

What presents itself to Madrick as good economic news, namely a recent fall in consumer debt and of the federal deficit, says nothing about those politically untamed economic players who are globally poised to profiteer from just about any economic scenario. It is simply implausible that the same corporate and financial stakeholders in the status quo model of economic growth will be flag-bearers for wage increases and greater income equality. Lasting remedies will not be found by returning to economic growth fuelled by new consumer spending on mostly superfluous goods. Our patterns of consumption, the purpose of economic growth as well as its social and environmental impacts and consequences, all need to be fundamentally questioned and revisited. If not, what's next? Perhaps 'Occupy the economists and their institutes'?

Glenn Brigaldino

Ottawa, 11 April 2013

(B)

UnHarperian

In a first-hand of account of how an ordinary, not necessarily mainstream citizen finds himself engulfed in the intrusive meddling of an increasingly unaccountable state security apparatus , William Vollmann   ["Life as a terrorist", September 2013] shares his experiences of how his civil rights have been intruded upon by his own government.

As one reads on, the narrative becomes regrettably diminished as it turns overly self-centered. What starts as an alarming account of the truly Orwellian state of affairs with regard to personal liberties and democratic freedoms in post-cold War western democracies, notably in the US, develops traits of a page filler. Such short-comings of style could easily be tolerated and simply be dismissed as the authorial technique Vollmann uses to impress upon the reader, the troublesome heights systematic surveillance of citizens have reached in the United States.

What eventually spoils, at least my own initially deeper sympathy with Vollmann and his account of the injustices inflicted upon him by the state's investigation agencies, might have merely been a slip of tongue, not necessarily an entrenched belief or conviction of his. But yes, Germans during the Nazi regime, many of them eager to 'be a good German' in Vollmann's words, were eager to spy and denounce suspected and real opponents of the dictatorship. My own grandfather's brother Arno, as a member of the communist party, became a victim of such betrayal by civilian opportunists. After two years in concentration camps, at the age of forty-two, he was eventually murdered in Dachau in 1940: hit on the back of the head with a shovel, it was secretly rumored.

Just as Vollmann speaks of 'UnAmericans', those persons with some, often only minuscule degree of state authority but who readily implement undemocratic government intrusions into citizens lives, in his next essay he way wish to keep in mind, that there were and still are 'UnGermans', just as there are 'UnIranians', 'UnChinese' or even 'UnCanadians', today. John Steinbeck certainly knew that.

Glenn Brigaldino, Ottawa Sept. 7th, 2013

Watertown, upstate New York
© 2013, Glenn Brigaldino